MW01113604

THIS PLANNER BOOK BELONGS TO:

NAME ● _____

CONTACT ● _____

EMAIL ● _____

YEAR TO VIEW..

JULY 2019

S	M	T	W	T	F	S
30	1	2	3	4	5	6
7	8	9	10	11	12	13
14	15	16	17	18	19	20
21	22	23	24	25	26	27
28	29	30	31	1	2	3
4	5	6	7	8	9	10

4 Independence Day

AUGUST 2019

S	M	T	W	T	F	S
28	29	30	31	1	2	3
4	5	6	7	8	9	10
11	12	13	14	15	16	17
18	19	20	21	22	23	24
25	26	27	28	29	30	31
1	2	3	4	5	6	7

SEPTEMBER 2019

S	M	T	W	T	F	S
1	2	3	4	5	6	7
8	9	10	11	12	13	14
15	16	17	18	19	20	21
22	23	24	25	26	27	28
29	30	1	2	3	4	5
6	7	8	9	10	11	12

2 Labor Day

OCTOBER 2019

S	M	T	W	T	F	S
29	30	1	2	3	4	5
6	7	8	9	10	11	12
13	14	15	16	17	18	19
20	21	22	23	24	25	26
27	28	29	30	31	1	2
3	4	5	6	7	8	9

14 Columbus Day

31 Halloween

NOVEMBER 2019

S	M	T	W	T	F	S
27	28	29	30	31	1	2
3	4	5	6	7	8	9
10	11	12	13	14	15	16
17	18	19	20	21	22	23
24	25	26	27	28	29	30
1	2	3	4	5	6	7

28 Thanksgiving

DECEMBER 2019

S	M	T	W	T	F	S
1	2	3	4	5	6	7
8	9	10	11	12	13	14
15	16	17	18	19	20	21
22	23	24	25	26	27	28
29	30	31	1	2	3	4
5	6	7	8	9	10	11

25 Christmas Day

JANUARY 2020

S	M	T	W	T	F	S
29	30	31	1	2	3	4
5	6	7	8	9	10	11
12	13	14	15	16	17	18
19	20	21	22	23	24	25
26	27	28	29	30	31	1
2	3	4	5	6	7	8

1 New Year's Day

20 Martin Luther King Jr. Day

FEBRUARY 2020

S	M	T	W	T	F	S
26	27	28	29	30	31	1
2	3	4	5	6	7	8
9	10	11	12	13	14	15
16	17	18	19	20	21	22
23	24	25	26	27	28	29
1	2	3	4	5	6	7

14 Valentine's Day

17 Presidents' Day

MARCH 2020

S	M	T	W	T	F	S
1	2	3	4	5	6	7
8	9	10	11	12	13	14
15	16	17	18	19	20	21
22	23	24	25	26	27	28
29	30	31	1	2	3	4
5	6	7	8	9	10	11

17 St. Patrick's Day

APRIL 2020

S	M	T	W	T	F	S
29	30	31	1	2	3	4
5	6	7	8	9	10	11
12	13	14	15	16	17	18
19	20	21	22	23	24	25
26	27	28	29	30	1	2
3	4	5	6	7	8	9

1 April Fools' Day

MAY 2020

S	M	T	W	T	F	S
26	27	28	29	30	1	2
3	4	5	6	7	8	9
10	11	12	13	14	15	16
17	18	19	20	21	22	23
24	25	26	27	28	29	30
31	1	2	3	4	5	6

10 Mother's Day

25 Memorial Day

JUNE 2020

S	M	T	W	T	F	S
31	1	2	3	4	5	6
7	8	9	10	11	12	13
14	15	16	17	18	19	20
21	22	23	24	25	26	27
28	29	30	1	2	3	4
5	6	7	8	9	10	11

21 Father's Day

Important Dates

Life Focus

July 2019

Sunday	Monday	Tuesday	Wednesday
30	1	2	3
7	8	9	10
14	15	16	17
21	22	23	24
28	29	30	31

"Anyone who has never made a mistake has never tried anything new."

Albert Einstein

Thursday	Friday	Saturday	- NOTES -
4 - Independence Day -	5	6	
11	12	13	
18	19	20	
25	26	27	
1	2	3	

JULY 2019

S	M	T	W	T	F	S
30	1	2	3	4	5	6
7	8	9	10	11	12	13
14	15	16	17	18	19	20
21	22	23	24	25	26	27
28	29	30	31	1	2	3
4	5	6	7	8	9	10

4 Independence Day

- THIS WEEK NOTES -

- FOCUS LIST ON THE WEEK -

☐
☐
☐

- NOTES -

SUN • 30th June 2019

- TO DO LIST -

☐
☐
☐
☐
☐

- NOTES -

MON • 1st July 2019

- TO DO LIST -

☐
☐
☐
☐
☐

- NOTES -

TUE • 2nd July 2019

- TO DO LIST -

☐
☐
☐
☐
☐

WED • 3rd July 2019

- TO DO LIST -

- [ ]
- [ ]
- [ ]
- [ ]
- [ ]

THU • 4th July 2019

• Independence Day

- TO DO LIST -

- [ ]
- [ ]
- [ ]
- [ ]
- [ ]

FRI • 5th July 2019

- TO DO LIST -

- [ ]
- [ ]
- [ ]
- [ ]
- [ ]

SAT • 6th July 2019

- TO DO LIST -

- [ ]
- [ ]
- [ ]
- [ ]
- [ ]

- NOTES -

- NOTES -

- NOTES -

- NOTES -

JULY 2019

S	M	T	W	T	F	S
30	1	2	3	4	5	6
7	8	9	10	11	12	13
14	15	16	17	18	19	20
21	22	23	24	25	26	27
28	29	30	31	1	2	3
4	5	6	7	8	9	10

4   Independence Day

- THIS WEEK NOTES -

- FOCUS LIST ON THE WEEK -
- [ ]
- [ ]
- [ ]

SUN • 7th July 2019

- TO DO LIST -
- [ ]
- [ ]
- [ ]
- [ ]
- [ ]

- NOTES -

MON • 8th July 2019

- TO DO LIST -
- [ ]
- [ ]
- [ ]
- [ ]
- [ ]

- NOTES -

TUE • 9th July 2019

- TO DO LIST -
- [ ]
- [ ]
- [ ]
- [ ]
- [ ]

- NOTES -

WED • 10th July 2019

- TO DO LIST -

- [ ]
- [ ]
- [ ]
- [ ]
- [ ]

THU • 11th July 2019

- TO DO LIST -

- [ ]
- [ ]
- [ ]
- [ ]
- [ ]

FRI • 12th July 2019

- TO DO LIST -

- [ ]
- [ ]
- [ ]
- [ ]
- [ ]

SAT • 13th July 2019

- TO DO LIST -

- [ ]
- [ ]
- [ ]
- [ ]
- [ ]

JULY 2019

S	M	T	W	T	F	S
30	1	2	3	4	5	6
7	8	9	10	11	12	13
14	15	16	17	18	19	20
21	22	23	24	25	26	27
28	29	30	31	1	2	3
4	5	6	7	8	9	10

4 Independence Day

- THIS WEEK NOTES -

- FOCUS LIST ON THE WEEK -

☐
☐
☐

SUN • 14th July 2019

- TO DO LIST -

☐
☐
☐
☐
☐

- NOTES -

MON • 15th July 2019

- TO DO LIST -

☐
☐
☐
☐
☐

- NOTES -

TUE • 16th July 2019

- TO DO LIST -

☐
☐
☐
☐
☐

- NOTES -

WED • 17th July 2019

- TO DO LIST -

☐ _____
☐ _____
☐ _____
☐ _____
☐ _____

- NOTES -

_____
_____
_____
_____
_____
_____
_____

THU • 18th July 2019

- TO DO LIST -

☐ _____
☐ _____
☐ _____
☐ _____
☐ _____

- NOTES -

_____
_____
_____
_____
_____
_____
_____

FRI • 19th July 2019

- TO DO LIST -

☐ _____
☐ _____
☐ _____
☐ _____
☐ _____

- NOTES -

_____
_____
_____
_____
_____
_____
_____

SAT • 20th July 2019

- TO DO LIST -

☐ _____
☐ _____
☐ _____
☐ _____
☐ _____

- NOTES -

_____
_____
_____
_____
_____
_____
_____

JULY 2019

S	M	T	W	T	F	S
30	1	2	3	4	5	6
7	8	9	10	11	12	13
14	15	16	17	18	19	20
21	22	23	24	25	26	27
28	29	30	31	1	2	3
4	5	6	7	8	9	10

4 Independence Day

- THIS WEEK NOTES -

- FOCUS LIST ON THE WEEK -

SUN • 21st July 2019

- TO DO LIST -

- NOTES -

MON • 22nd July 2019

- TO DO LIST -

- NOTES -

TUE • 23rd July 2019

- TO DO LIST -

- NOTES -

WED • 24th July 2019

- TO DO LIST -

☐
☐
☐
☐
☐

THU • 25th July 2019

- TO DO LIST -

☐
☐
☐
☐
☐

FRI • 26th July 2019

- TO DO LIST -

☐
☐
☐
☐
☐

SAT • 27th July 2019

- TO DO LIST -

☐
☐
☐
☐
☐

JULY 2019

S	M	T	W	T	F	S
30	1	2	3	4	5	6
7	8	9	10	11	12	13
14	15	16	17	18	19	20
21	22	23	24	25	26	27
28	29	30	31	1	2	3
4	5	6	7	8	9	10

4   Independence Day

- THIS WEEK NOTES -

- FOCUS LIST ON THE WEEK -

☐
☐
☐

- NOTES -

SUN • 28th July 2019

- TO DO LIST -

☐
☐
☐
☐
☐

- NOTES -

MON • 29th July 2019

- TO DO LIST -

☐
☐
☐
☐
☐

- NOTES -

TUE • 30th July 2019

- TO DO LIST -

☐
☐
☐
☐
☐

WED • 31st July 2019

- TO DO LIST -

- [ ]
- [ ]
- [ ]
- [ ]
- [ ]

THU • 1st August 2019

- TO DO LIST -

- [ ]
- [ ]
- [ ]
- [ ]
- [ ]

FRI • 2nd August 2019

- TO DO LIST -

- [ ]
- [ ]
- [ ]
- [ ]
- [ ]

SAT • 3rd August 2019

- TO DO LIST -

- [ ]
- [ ]
- [ ]
- [ ]
- [ ]

August 2019

Sunday	Monday	Tuesday	Wednesday
28	29	30	31
4	5	6	7
11	12	13	14
18	19	20	21
25	26	27	28

"But I know, somehow, that
only when it is dark enough can you see the stars."
Martin Luther King Jr.

Thursday	Friday	Saturday	- NOTES -
1	2	3	
8	9	10	
15	16	17	
22	23	24	
29	30	31	

AUGUST 2019

S	M	T	W	T	F	S
28	29	30	31	1	2	3
4	5	6	7	8	9	10
11	12	13	14	15	16	17
18	19	20	21	22	23	24
25	26	27	28	29	30	31
1	2	3	4	5	6	7

- THIS WEEK NOTES -

- FOCUS LIST ON THE WEEK -

☐ ....

☐ ....

☐ ....

- NOTES -

SUN • 4th August 2019

- TO DO LIST -

☐

☐

☐

☐

☐

- NOTES -

MON • 5th August 2019

- TO DO LIST -

☐

☐

☐

☐

☐

- NOTES -

TUE • 6th August 2019

- TO DO LIST -

☐

☐

☐

☐

☐

WED • 7th August 2019

- TO DO LIST -

☐ ....
☐ ....
☐ ....
☐ ....
☐ ....

- NOTES -

THU • 8th August 2019

- TO DO LIST -

☐ ....
☐ ....
☐ ....
☐ ....
☐ ....

- NOTES -

FRI • 9th August 2019

- TO DO LIST -

☐ ....
☐ ....
☐ ....
☐ ....
☐ ....

- NOTES -

SAT • 10th August 2019

- TO DO LIST -

☐ ....
☐ ....
☐ ....
☐ ....
☐ ....

- NOTES -

AUGUST 2019

S	M	T	W	T	F	S
28	29	30	31	1	2	3
4	5	6	7	8	9	10
11	12	13	14	15	16	17
18	19	20	21	22	23	24
25	26	27	28	29	30	31
1	2	3	4	5	6	7

- THIS WEEK NOTES -

- FOCUS LIST ON THE WEEK -

☐
☐
☐

- NOTES -

SUN • 11th August 2019

- TO DO LIST -

☐
☐
☐
☐
☐

- NOTES -

MON • 12th August 2019

- TO DO LIST -

☐
☐
☐
☐
☐

- NOTES -

TUE • 13th August 2019

- TO DO LIST -

☐
☐
☐
☐
☐

WED • 14th August 2019

- TO DO LIST -

- [ ]
- [ ]
- [ ]
- [ ]
- [ ]

- NOTES -

THU • 15th August 2019

- TO DO LIST -

- [ ]
- [ ]
- [ ]
- [ ]
- [ ]

- NOTES -

FRI • 16th August 2019

- TO DO LIST -

- [ ]
- [ ]
- [ ]
- [ ]
- [ ]

- NOTES -

SAT • 17th August 2019

- TO DO LIST -

- [ ]
- [ ]
- [ ]
- [ ]
- [ ]

- NOTES -

AUGUST 2019

S	M	T	W	T	F	S
28	29	30	31	1	2	3
4	5	6	7	8	9	10
11	12	13	14	15	16	17
18	19	20	21	22	23	24
25	26	27	28	29	30	31
1	2	3	4	5	6	7

- THIS WEEK NOTES -

- FOCUS LIST ON THE WEEK -

☐ _____

☐ _____

☐ _____

SUN • 18th August 2019

- TO DO LIST -

☐ _____

☐ _____

☐ _____

☐ _____

☐ _____

- NOTES -

MON • 19th August 2019

- TO DO LIST -

☐ _____

☐ _____

☐ _____

☐ _____

☐ _____

- NOTES -

TUE • 20th August 2019

- TO DO LIST -

☐ _____

☐ _____

☐ _____

☐ _____

☐ _____

- NOTES -

WED • 21st August 2019

- TO DO LIST -

- [ ]
- [ ]
- [ ]
- [ ]
- [ ]

THU • 22nd August 2019

- TO DO LIST -

- [ ]
- [ ]
- [ ]
- [ ]
- [ ]

- NOTES -

FRI • 23rd August 2019

- TO DO LIST -

- [ ]
- [ ]
- [ ]
- [ ]
- [ ]

- NOTES -

SAT • 24th August 2019

- TO DO LIST -

- [ ]
- [ ]
- [ ]
- [ ]
- [ ]

- NOTES -

AUGUST 2019

S	M	T	W	T	F	S
28	29	30	31	1	2	3
4	5	6	7	8	9	10
11	12	13	14	15	16	17
18	19	20	21	22	23	24
25	26	27	28	29	30	31
1	2	3	4	5	6	7

- THIS WEEK NOTES -

- FOCUS LIST ON THE WEEK -

- NOTES -

SUN • 25th August 2019

- TO DO LIST -

- NOTES -

MON • 26th August 2019

- TO DO LIST -

- NOTES -

TUE • 27th August 2019

- TO DO LIST -

WED • 28th August 2019

- TO DO LIST -

- [ ]
- [ ]
- [ ]
- [ ]
- [ ]

- NOTES -

THU • 29th August 2019

- TO DO LIST -

- [ ]
- [ ]
- [ ]
- [ ]
- [ ]

- NOTES -

FRI • 30th August 2019

- TO DO LIST -

- [ ]
- [ ]
- [ ]
- [ ]
- [ ]

- NOTES -

SAT • 31st August 2019

- TO DO LIST -

- [ ]
- [ ]
- [ ]
- [ ]
- [ ]

- NOTES -

September 2019

Sunday	Monday	Tuesday	Wednesday
1	2 - Labor Day -	3	4
8	9	10	11
15	16	17	18
22	23	24	25
29	30	1	2

Thursday	Friday	Saturday	- NOTES -
5	6	7	
12	13	14	
19	20	21	
26	27	28	
3	4	5	

SEPTEMBER 2019

S	M	T	W	T	F	S
1	2	3	4	5	6	7
8	9	10	11	12	13	14
15	16	17	18	19	20	21
22	23	24	25	26	27	28
29	30	1	2	3	4	5
6	7	8	9	10	11	12

2 Labor Day

- THIS WEEK NOTES -

- FOCUS LIST ON THE WEEK -

☐

☐

☐

- NOTES -

SUN • 1st September 2019

- TO DO LIST -

☐
☐
☐
☐
☐

- NOTES -

MON • 2nd September 2019

• Labor Day

- TO DO LIST -

☐
☐
☐
☐
☐

- NOTES -

TUE • 3rd September 2019

- TO DO LIST -

☐
☐
☐
☐
☐

WED • 4th September 2019

- NOTES -

- TO DO LIST -

- [ ]
- [ ]
- [ ]
- [ ]
- [ ]

THU • 5th September 2019

- NOTES -

- TO DO LIST -

- [ ]
- [ ]
- [ ]
- [ ]
- [ ]

FRI • 6th September 2019

- NOTES -

- TO DO LIST -

- [ ]
- [ ]
- [ ]
- [ ]
- [ ]

SAT • 7th September 2019

- NOTES -

- TO DO LIST -

- [ ]
- [ ]
- [ ]
- [ ]
- [ ]

SEPTEMBER 2019

S	M	T	W	T	F	S
1	2	3	4	5	6	7
8	9	10	11	12	13	14
15	16	17	18	19	20	21
22	23	24	25	26	27	28
29	30	1	2	3	4	5
6	7	8	9	10	11	12

2 Labor Day

- THIS WEEK NOTES -

- FOCUS LIST ON THE WEEK -

☐

☐

☐

SUN • 8th September 2019

- TO DO LIST -

☐

☐

☐

☐

☐

- NOTES -

MON • 9th September 2019

- TO DO LIST -

☐

☐

☐

☐

☐

- NOTES -

TUE • 10th September 2019

- TO DO LIST -

☐

☐

☐

☐

☐

- NOTES -

WED • 11th September 2019

- TO DO LIST -

- [ ]
- [ ]
- [ ]
- [ ]
- [ ]

- NOTES -

THU • 12th September 2019

- TO DO LIST -

- [ ]
- [ ]
- [ ]
- [ ]
- [ ]

- NOTES -

FRI • 13th September 2019

- TO DO LIST -

- [ ]
- [ ]
- [ ]
- [ ]
- [ ]

- NOTES -

SAT • 14th September 2019

- TO DO LIST -

- [ ]
- [ ]
- [ ]
- [ ]
- [ ]

- NOTES -

SEPTEMBER 2019

S	M	T	W	T	F	S
1	2	3	4	5	6	7
8	9	10	11	12	13	14
15	16	17	18	19	20	21
22	23	24	25	26	27	28
29	30	1	2	3	4	5
6	7	8	9	10	11	12

2 Labor Day

- THIS WEEK NOTES -

- FOCUS LIST ON THE WEEK -

☐
☐
☐

- NOTES -

SUN • 15th September 2019

- TO DO LIST -

☐
☐
☐
☐
☐

- NOTES -

MON • 16th September 2019

- TO DO LIST -

☐
☐
☐
☐
☐

- NOTES -

TUE • 17th September 2019

- TO DO LIST -

☐
☐
☐
☐
☐

WED • 18th September 2019

- TO DO LIST -

- [ ]
- [ ]
- [ ]
- [ ]
- [ ]

THU • 19th September 2019

- NOTES -

- TO DO LIST -

- [ ]
- [ ]
- [ ]
- [ ]
- [ ]

FRI • 20th September 2019

- NOTES -

- TO DO LIST -

- [ ]
- [ ]
- [ ]
- [ ]
- [ ]

SAT • 21st September 2019

- NOTES -

- TO DO LIST -

- [ ]
- [ ]
- [ ]
- [ ]
- [ ]

SEPTEMBER 2019

S	M	T	W	T	F	S
1	2	3	4	5	6	7
8	9	10	11	12	13	14
15	16	17	18	19	20	21
22	23	24	25	26	27	28
29	30	1	2	3	4	5
6	7	8	9	10	11	12

2   Labor Day

- THIS WEEK NOTES -

- FOCUS LIST ON THE WEEK -

☐
☐
☐

SUN • 22nd September 2019

- TO DO LIST -

☐
☐
☐
☐
☐

- NOTES -

MON • 23rd September 2019

- TO DO LIST -

☐
☐
☐
☐
☐

- NOTES -

TUE • 24th September 2019

- TO DO LIST -

☐
☐
☐
☐
☐

- NOTES -

WED • 25th September 2019

- TO DO LIST -

- [ ]
- [ ]
- [ ]
- [ ]
- [ ]

THU • 26th September 2019

- NOTES -

- TO DO LIST -

- [ ]
- [ ]
- [ ]
- [ ]
- [ ]

FRI • 27th September 2019

- NOTES -

- TO DO LIST -

- [ ]
- [ ]
- [ ]
- [ ]
- [ ]

SAT • 28th September 2019

- NOTES -

- TO DO LIST -

- [ ]
- [ ]
- [ ]
- [ ]
- [ ]

SEPTEMBER 2019

S	M	T	W	T	F	S
1	2	3	4	5	6	7
8	9	10	11	12	13	14
15	16	17	18	19	20	21
22	23	24	25	26	27	28
29	30	1	2	3	4	5
6	7	8	9	10	11	12

2 Labor Day

- THIS WEEK NOTES -

- FOCUS LIST ON THE WEEK -

☐
☐
☐

SUN • 29th September 2019

- TO DO LIST -

☐
☐
☐
☐
☐

- NOTES -

MON • 30th September 2019

- TO DO LIST -

☐
☐
☐
☐
☐

- NOTES -

TUE • 1st October 2019

- TO DO LIST -

☐
☐
☐
☐
☐

- NOTES -

WED • 2nd October 2019

- TO DO LIST -

- [ ]
- [ ]
- [ ]
- [ ]
- [ ]

THU • 3rd October 2019

- TO DO LIST -

- [ ]
- [ ]
- [ ]
- [ ]
- [ ]

FRI • 4th October 2019

- TO DO LIST -

- [ ]
- [ ]
- [ ]
- [ ]
- [ ]

SAT • 5th October 2019

- TO DO LIST -

- [ ]
- [ ]
- [ ]
- [ ]
- [ ]

October 2019

Sunday	Monday	Tuesday	Wednesday
29	30	1	2
6	7	8	9
13	14 - Columbus Day -	15	16
20	21	22	23
27	28	29	30

Thursday	Friday	Saturday	- NOTES -
3	4	5	
10	11	12	
17	18	19	
24	25	26	
31 - Halloween -	1	2	

OCTOBER 2019

S	M	T	W	T	F	S
29	30	1	2	3	4	5
6	7	8	9	10	11	12
13	14	15	16	17	18	19
20	21	22	23	24	25	26
27	28	29	30	31	1	2
3	4	5	6	7	8	9

14 Columbus Day
31 Halloween

- THIS WEEK NOTES -

- FOCUS LIST ON THE WEEK -

☐
☐
☐

SUN • 6th October 2019

- TO DO LIST -

☐
☐
☐
☐
☐

- NOTES -

MON • 7th October 2019

- TO DO LIST -

☐
☐
☐
☐
☐

- NOTES -

TUE • 8th October 2019

- TO DO LIST -

☐
☐
☐
☐
☐

- NOTES -

WED • 9th October 2019

- TO DO LIST -

- [ ]
- [ ]
- [ ]
- [ ]
- [ ]

- NOTES -

THU • 10th October 2019

- TO DO LIST -

- [ ]
- [ ]
- [ ]
- [ ]
- [ ]

- NOTES -

FRI • 11th October 2019

- TO DO LIST -

- [ ]
- [ ]
- [ ]
- [ ]
- [ ]

- NOTES -

SAT • 12th October 2019

- TO DO LIST -

- [ ]
- [ ]
- [ ]
- [ ]
- [ ]

- NOTES -

OCTOBER 2019

S	M	T	W	T	F	S
29	30	1	2	3	4	5
6	7	8	9	10	11	12
13	14	15	16	17	18	19
20	21	22	23	24	25	26
27	28	29	30	31	1	2
3	4	5	6	7	8	9

14 Columbus Day
31 Halloween

- THIS WEEK NOTES -

- FOCUS LIST ON THE WEEK -
- ☐
- ☐
- ☐

SUN • 13th October 2019

- NOTES -

- TO DO LIST -

☐
☐
☐
☐
☐

MON • 14th October 2019

• Columbus Day

- NOTES -

- TO DO LIST -

☐
☐
☐
☐
☐

TUE • 15th October 2019

- NOTES -

- TO DO LIST -

☐
☐
☐
☐
☐

WED • 16th October 2019

- TO DO LIST -

☐ ....
☐ ....
☐ ....
☐ ....
☐ ....

THU • 17th October 2019

- TO DO LIST -

☐ ....
☐ ....
☐ ....
☐ ....
☐ ....

FRI • 18th October 2019

- TO DO LIST -

☐ ....
☐ ....
☐ ....
☐ ....
☐ ....

SAT • 19th October 2019

- TO DO LIST -

☐ ....
☐ ....
☐ ....
☐ ....
☐ ....

OCTOBER 2019

S	M	T	W	T	F	S
29	30	1	2	3	4	5
6	7	8	9	10	11	12
13	14	15	16	17	18	19
20	21	22	23	24	25	26
27	28	29	30	31	1	2
3	4	5	6	7	8	9

14 Columbus Day
31 Halloween

- THIS WEEK NOTES -

- FOCUS LIST ON THE WEEK -
- [ ]
- [ ]
- [ ]

SUN • 20th October 2019

- TO DO LIST -

- [ ]
- [ ]
- [ ]
- [ ]
- [ ]

- NOTES -

MON • 21st October 2019

- TO DO LIST -

- [ ]
- [ ]
- [ ]
- [ ]
- [ ]

- NOTES -

TUE • 22nd October 2019

- TO DO LIST -

- [ ]
- [ ]
- [ ]
- [ ]
- [ ]

- NOTES -

WED • 23rd October 2019

- TO DO LIST -

- [ ]
- [ ]
- [ ]
- [ ]
- [ ]

THU • 24th October 2019

- TO DO LIST -

- [ ]
- [ ]
- [ ]
- [ ]
- [ ]

FRI • 25th October 2019

- TO DO LIST -

- [ ]
- [ ]
- [ ]
- [ ]
- [ ]

SAT • 26th October 2019

- TO DO LIST -

- [ ]
- [ ]
- [ ]
- [ ]
- [ ]

OCTOBER 2019

S	M	T	W	T	F	S
29	30	1	2	3	4	5
6	7	8	9	10	11	12
13	14	15	16	17	18	19
20	21	22	23	24	25	26
27	28	29	30	31	1	2
3	4	5	6	7	8	9

14 Columbus Day
31 Halloween

- THIS WEEK NOTES -

- FOCUS LIST ON THE WEEK -

☐
☐
☐

- NOTES -

SUN • 27th October 2019

- TO DO LIST -

☐
☐
☐
☐
☐

- NOTES -

MON • 28th October 2019

- TO DO LIST -

☐
☐
☐
☐
☐

- NOTES -

TUE • 29th October 2019

- TO DO LIST -

☐
☐
☐
☐
☐

WED • 30th October 2019

- TO DO LIST -

☐
☐
☐
☐
☐

THU • 31st October 2019

• Halloween

- TO DO LIST -

☐
☐
☐
☐
☐

FRI • 1st November 2019

- TO DO LIST -

☐
☐
☐
☐
☐

SAT • 2nd November 2019

- TO DO LIST -

☐
☐
☐
☐
☐

November 2019

Sunday	Monday	Tuesday	Wednesday
27	28	29	30
3	4	5	6
10	11	12	13
17	18	19	20
24	25	26	27

"Success is not final, failure is not fatal:
it is the courage to continue that counts."
Winston S. Churchill

Thursday	Friday	Saturday	- NOTES -
31	1	2	
7	8	9	
14	15	16	
21	22	23	
28	29	30	

- Thanksgiving -

NOVEMBER 2019

S	M	T	W	T	F	S
27	28	29	30	31	1	2
3	4	5	6	7	8	9
10	11	12	13	14	15	16
17	18	19	20	21	22	23
24	25	26	27	28	29	30
1	2	3	4	5	6	7

28 Thanksgiving

- THIS WEEK NOTES -

- FOCUS LIST ON THE WEEK -

- [ ]
- [ ]
- [ ]

- NOTES -

SUN • 3rd November 2019

- TO DO LIST -

- [ ]
- [ ]
- [ ]
- [ ]
- [ ]

- NOTES -

MON • 4th November 2019

- TO DO LIST -

- [ ]
- [ ]
- [ ]
- [ ]
- [ ]

- NOTES -

TUE • 5th November 2019

- TO DO LIST -

- [ ]
- [ ]
- [ ]
- [ ]
- [ ]

WED • 6th November 2019

- TO DO LIST -

- [ ]
- [ ]
- [ ]
- [ ]
- [ ]

THU • 7th November 2019

- NOTES -

- TO DO LIST -

- [ ]
- [ ]
- [ ]
- [ ]
- [ ]

FRI • 8th November 2019

- NOTES -

- TO DO LIST -

- [ ]
- [ ]
- [ ]
- [ ]
- [ ]

SAT • 9th November 2019

- NOTES -

- TO DO LIST -

- [ ]
- [ ]
- [ ]
- [ ]
- [ ]

NOVEMBER 2019

S	M	T	W	T	F	S
27	28	29	30	31	1	2
3	4	5	6	7	8	9
10	11	12	13	14	15	16
17	18	19	20	21	22	23
24	25	26	27	28	29	30
1	2	3	4	5	6	7

28 Thanksgiving

- THIS WEEK NOTES -

- FOCUS LIST ON THE WEEK -

☐
☐
☐

SUN • 10th November 2019

- TO DO LIST -

☐
☐
☐
☐
☐

- NOTES -

MON • 11th November 2019

- TO DO LIST -

☐
☐
☐
☐
☐

- NOTES -

TUE • 12th November 2019

- TO DO LIST -

☐
☐
☐
☐
☐

- NOTES -

WED • 13th November 2019

- TO DO LIST -

- [ ]
- [ ]
- [ ]
- [ ]
- [ ]

THU • 14th November 2019

- TO DO LIST -

- [ ]
- [ ]
- [ ]
- [ ]
- [ ]

FRI • 15th November 2019

- TO DO LIST -

- [ ]
- [ ]
- [ ]
- [ ]
- [ ]

SAT • 16th November 2019

- TO DO LIST -

- [ ]
- [ ]
- [ ]
- [ ]
- [ ]

NOVEMBER 2019

S	M	T	W	T	F	S
27	28	29	30	31	1	2
3	4	5	6	7	8	9
10	11	12	13	14	15	16
17	18	19	20	21	22	23
24	25	26	27	28	29	30
1	2	3	4	5	6	7

28 Thanksgiving

- THIS WEEK NOTES -

- FOCUS LIST ON THE WEEK -

☐

☐

☐

SUN • 17th November 2019

- TO DO LIST -

☐
☐
☐
☐
☐

- NOTES -

MON • 18th November 2019

- TO DO LIST -

☐
☐
☐
☐
☐

- NOTES -

TUE • 19th November 2019

- TO DO LIST -

☐
☐
☐
☐
☐

- NOTES -

WED • 20th November 2019

- TO DO LIST -

☐
☐
☐
☐
☐

THU • 21st November 2019

- TO DO LIST -

☐
☐
☐
☐
☐

FRI • 22nd November 2019

- TO DO LIST -

☐
☐
☐
☐
☐

SAT • 23rd November 2019

- TO DO LIST -

☐
☐
☐
☐
☐

NOVEMBER 2019

S	M	T	W	T	F	S
27	28	29	30	31	1	2
3	4	5	6	7	8	9
10	11	12	13	14	15	16
17	18	19	20	21	22	23
24	25	26	27	28	29	30
1	2	3	4	5	6	7

28 Thanksgiving

- THIS WEEK NOTES -

- FOCUS LIST ON THE WEEK -

☐
☐
☐

SUN • 24th November 2019

- TO DO LIST -

☐
☐
☐
☐
☐

- NOTES -

MON • 25th November 2019

- TO DO LIST -

☐
☐
☐
☐
☐

- NOTES -

TUE • 26th November 2019

- TO DO LIST -

☐
☐
☐
☐
☐

- NOTES -

WED • 27th November 2019

- TO DO LIST -

- [ ]
- [ ]
- [ ]
- [ ]
- [ ]

- NOTES -

THU • 28th November 2019

• Thanksgiving

- TO DO LIST -

- [ ]
- [ ]
- [ ]
- [ ]
- [ ]

- NOTES -

FRI • 29th November 2019

- TO DO LIST -

- [ ]
- [ ]
- [ ]
- [ ]
- [ ]

- NOTES -

SAT • 30th November 2019

- TO DO LIST -

- [ ]
- [ ]
- [ ]
- [ ]
- [ ]

- NOTES -

December 2019

Sunday	Monday	Tuesday	Wednesday
1	2	3	4
8	9	10	11
15	16	17	18
22	23	24	25 - Christmas Day -
29	30	31	1

Thursday	Friday	Saturday
5	6	7
12	13	14
19	20	21
26	27	28
2	3	4

- NOTES -

DECEMBER 2019

S	M	T	W	T	F	S
1	2	3	4	5	6	7
8	9	10	11	12	13	14
15	16	17	18	19	20	21
22	23	24	25	26	27	28
29	30	31	1	2	3	4
5	6	7	8	9	10	11

25 Christmas Day

- THIS WEEK NOTES -

- FOCUS LIST ON THE WEEK -

☐
☐
☐

SUN • 1st December 2019

- TO DO LIST -

☐
☐
☐
☐
☐

- NOTES -

MON • 2nd December 2019

- TO DO LIST -

☐
☐
☐
☐
☐

- NOTES -

TUE • 3rd December 2019

- TO DO LIST -

☐
☐
☐
☐
☐

- NOTES -

WED • 4th December 2019

- TO DO LIST -
- [ ]
- [ ]
- [ ]
- [ ]
- [ ]

- NOTES -

THU • 5th December 2019

- TO DO LIST -
- [ ]
- [ ]
- [ ]
- [ ]
- [ ]

- NOTES -

FRI • 6th December 2019

- TO DO LIST -
- [ ]
- [ ]
- [ ]
- [ ]
- [ ]

- NOTES -

SAT • 7th December 2019

- TO DO LIST -
- [ ]
- [ ]
- [ ]
- [ ]
- [ ]

- NOTES -

DECEMBER 2019

S	M	T	W	T	F	S
1	2	3	4	5	6	7
8	9	10	11	12	13	14
15	16	17	18	19	20	21
22	23	24	25	26	27	28
29	30	31	1	2	3	4
5	6	7	8	9	10	11

25 Christmas Day

- THIS WEEK NOTES -

- FOCUS LIST ON THE WEEK -

☐

☐

☐

SUN • 8th December 2019

- TO DO LIST -

☐

☐

☐

☐

☐

- NOTES -

MON • 9th December 2019

- TO DO LIST -

☐

☐

☐

☐

☐

- NOTES -

TUE • 10th December 2019

- TO DO LIST -

☐

☐

☐

☐

☐

- NOTES -

WED • 11th December 2019

- TO DO LIST -

☐ _____
☐ _____
☐ _____
☐ _____
☐ _____

- NOTES -

_____
_____
_____
_____
_____
_____
_____

THU • 12th December 2019

- TO DO LIST -

☐ _____
☐ _____
☐ _____
☐ _____
☐ _____

- NOTES -

_____
_____
_____
_____
_____
_____
_____

FRI • 13th December 2019

- TO DO LIST -

☐ _____
☐ _____
☐ _____
☐ _____
☐ _____

- NOTES -

_____
_____
_____
_____
_____
_____
_____

SAT • 14th December 2019

- TO DO LIST -

☐ _____
☐ _____
☐ _____
☐ _____
☐ _____

- NOTES -

_____
_____
_____
_____
_____
_____
_____

DECEMBER 2019

S	M	T	W	T	F	S
1	2	3	4	5	6	7
8	9	10	11	12	13	14
15	16	17	18	19	20	21
22	23	24	25	26	27	28
29	30	31	1	2	3	4
5	6	7	8	9	10	11

25 Christmas Day

- THIS WEEK NOTES -

- FOCUS LIST ON THE WEEK -

☐ _____

☐ _____

☐ _____

SUN • 15th December 2019

- TO DO LIST -

☐ _____

☐ _____

☐ _____

☐ _____

☐ _____

- NOTES -

MON • 16th December 2019

- TO DO LIST -

☐ _____

☐ _____

☐ _____

☐ _____

☐ _____

- NOTES -

TUE • 17th December 2019

- TO DO LIST -

☐ _____

☐ _____

☐ _____

☐ _____

☐ _____

- NOTES -

WED • 18th December 2019

- TO DO LIST -

- [ ]
- [ ]
- [ ]
- [ ]
- [ ]

THU • 19th December 2019

- TO DO LIST -

- [ ]
- [ ]
- [ ]
- [ ]
- [ ]

FRI • 20th December 2019

- TO DO LIST -

- [ ]
- [ ]
- [ ]
- [ ]
- [ ]

SAT • 21st December 2019

- TO DO LIST -

- [ ]
- [ ]
- [ ]
- [ ]
- [ ]

DECEMBER 2019

S	M	T	W	T	F	S
1	2	3	4	5	6	7
8	9	10	11	12	13	14
15	16	17	18	19	20	21
22	23	24	25	26	27	28
29	30	31	1	2	3	4
5	6	7	8	9	10	11

25 Christmas Day

- THIS WEEK NOTES -

- FOCUS LIST ON THE WEEK -

☐ _____

☐ _____

☐ _____

SUN • 22nd December 2019

- TO DO LIST -

☐ _____

☐ _____

☐ _____

☐ _____

☐ _____

- NOTES -

MON • 23rd December 2019

- TO DO LIST -

☐ _____

☐ _____

☐ _____

☐ _____

☐ _____

- NOTES -

TUE • 24th December 2019

- TO DO LIST -

☐ _____

☐ _____

☐ _____

☐ _____

☐ _____

- NOTES -

WED • 25th December 2019

• Christmas Day

- TO DO LIST -

- [ ]
- [ ]
- [ ]
- [ ]
- [ ]

THU • 26th December 2019

- TO DO LIST -

- [ ]
- [ ]
- [ ]
- [ ]
- [ ]

FRI • 27th December 2019

- TO DO LIST -

- [ ]
- [ ]
- [ ]
- [ ]
- [ ]

SAT • 28th December 2019

- TO DO LIST -

- [ ]
- [ ]
- [ ]
- [ ]
- [ ]

DECEMBER 2019

S	M	T	W	T	F	S
1	2	3	4	5	6	7
8	9	10	11	12	13	14
15	16	17	18	19	20	21
22	23	24	25	26	27	28
29	30	31	1	2	3	4
5	6	7	8	9	10	11

25 Christmas Day

- THIS WEEK NOTES -

- FOCUS LIST ON THE WEEK -

☐

☐

☐

- NOTES -

SUN • 29th December 2019

- TO DO LIST -

☐

☐

☐

☐

☐

- NOTES -

MON • 30th December 2019

- TO DO LIST -

☐

☐

☐

☐

☐

- NOTES -

TUE • 31st December 2019

- TO DO LIST -

☐

☐

☐

☐

☐

WED • 1st January 2020

• New Year's Day

- TO DO LIST -

- [ ]
- [ ]
- [ ]
- [ ]
- [ ]

THU • 2nd January 2020

- TO DO LIST -

- [ ]
- [ ]
- [ ]
- [ ]
- [ ]

FRI • 3rd January 2020

- TO DO LIST -

- [ ]
- [ ]
- [ ]
- [ ]
- [ ]

SAT • 4th January 2020

- TO DO LIST -

- [ ]
- [ ]
- [ ]
- [ ]
- [ ]

January 2020

Sunday	Monday	Tuesday	Wednesday
29	30	31	1 - New Year's Day -
5	6	7	8
12	13	14	15
19	20 - Martin Luther King Jr. Day -	21	22
26	27	28	29

"Nothing is impossible, the word itself says 'I'm possible'!"

Audrey Hepburn

Thursday	Friday	Saturday	- NOTES -
2	3	4	
9	10	11	
16	17	18	
23	24	25	
30	31	1	

JANUARY 2020

S	M	T	W	T	F	S
29	30	31	1	2	3	4
5	6	7	8	9	10	11
12	13	14	15	16	17	18
19	20	21	22	23	24	25
26	27	28	29	30	31	1
2	3	4	5	6	7	8

1 New Year's Day
20 Martin Luther King Jr. Day

- THIS WEEK NOTES -

- FOCUS LIST ON THE WEEK -

☐

☐

☐

SUN • 5th January 2020

- TO DO LIST -

☐

☐

☐

☐

☐

- NOTES -

MON • 6th January 2020

- TO DO LIST -

☐

☐

☐

☐

☐

- NOTES -

TUE • 7th January 2020

- TO DO LIST -

☐

☐

☐

☐

☐

- NOTES -

WED • 8th January 2020

- TO DO LIST -

- [ ]
- [ ]
- [ ]
- [ ]
- [ ]

THU • 9th January 2020

- NOTES -

- TO DO LIST -

- [ ]
- [ ]
- [ ]
- [ ]
- [ ]

FRI • 10th January 2020

- NOTES -

- TO DO LIST -

- [ ]
- [ ]
- [ ]
- [ ]
- [ ]

SAT • 11th January 2020

- NOTES -

- TO DO LIST -

- [ ]
- [ ]
- [ ]
- [ ]
- [ ]

JANUARY 2020

S	M	T	W	T	F	S
29	30	31	1	2	3	4
5	6	7	8	9	10	11
12	13	14	15	16	17	18
19	20	21	22	23	24	25
26	27	28	29	30	31	1
2	3	4	5	6	7	8

1 New Year's Day
20 Martin Luther King Jr. Day

- THIS WEEK NOTES -

- FOCUS LIST ON THE WEEK -

☐
☐
☐

SUN • 12th January 2020

- TO DO LIST -

☐
☐
☐
☐
☐

- NOTES -

MON • 13th January 2020

- TO DO LIST -

☐
☐
☐
☐
☐

- NOTES -

TUE • 14th January 2020

- TO DO LIST -

☐
☐
☐
☐
☐

- NOTES -

WED • 15th January 2020

- [ ]
- [ ]
- [ ]
- [ ]
- [ ]

THU • 16th January 2020

- [ ]
- [ ]
- [ ]
- [ ]
- [ ]

FRI • 17th January 2020

- [ ]
- [ ]
- [ ]
- [ ]
- [ ]

SAT • 18th January 2020

- [ ]
- [ ]
- [ ]
- [ ]
- [ ]

JANUARY 2020

S	M	T	W	T	F	S
29	30	31	1	2	3	4
5	6	7	8	9	10	11
12	13	14	15	16	17	18
19	20	21	22	23	24	25
26	27	28	29	30	31	1
2	3	4	5	6	7	8

1 New Year's Day
20 Martin Luther King Jr. Day

- THIS WEEK NOTES -

- FOCUS LIST ON THE WEEK -
- ☐ ....
- ☐ ....
- ☐ ....

SUN • 19th January 2020

- TO DO LIST -

- ☐
- ☐
- ☐
- ☐
- ☐

- NOTES -

MON • 20th January 2020

• Martin Luther King Jr. Day

- TO DO LIST -

- ☐
- ☐
- ☐
- ☐
- ☐

- NOTES -

TUE • 21st January 2020

- TO DO LIST -

- ☐
- ☐
- ☐
- ☐
- ☐

- NOTES -

WED • 22nd January 2020

- TO DO LIST -

- [ ]
- [ ]
- [ ]
- [ ]
- [ ]

THU • 23rd January 2020

- NOTES -

- TO DO LIST -

- [ ]
- [ ]
- [ ]
- [ ]
- [ ]

FRI • 24th January 2020

- NOTES -

- TO DO LIST -

- [ ]
- [ ]
- [ ]
- [ ]
- [ ]

SAT • 25th January 2020

- NOTES -

- TO DO LIST -

- [ ]
- [ ]
- [ ]
- [ ]
- [ ]

JANUARY 2020

S	M	T	W	T	F	S
29	30	31	1	2	3	4
5	6	7	8	9	10	11
12	13	14	15	16	17	18
19	20	21	22	23	24	25
26	27	28	29	30	31	1
2	3	4	5	6	7	8

1 New Year's Day
20 Martin Luther King Jr. Day

- THIS WEEK NOTES -

- FOCUS LIST ON THE WEEK -

☐ ....
☐ ....
☐ ....

SUN • 26th January 2020

- TO DO LIST -

☐ ....
☐ ....
☐ ....
☐ ....
☐ ....

- NOTES -

MON • 27th January 2020

- TO DO LIST -

☐ ....
☐ ....
☐ ....
☐ ....
☐ ....

- NOTES -

TUE • 28th January 2020

- TO DO LIST -

☐ ....
☐ ....
☐ ....
☐ ....
☐ ....

- NOTES -

WED • 29th January 2020

- TO DO LIST -

- [ ]
- [ ]
- [ ]
- [ ]
- [ ]

- NOTES -

THU • 30th January 2020

- TO DO LIST -

- [ ]
- [ ]
- [ ]
- [ ]
- [ ]

- NOTES -

FRI • 31st January 2020

- TO DO LIST -

- [ ]
- [ ]
- [ ]
- [ ]
- [ ]

- NOTES -

SAT • 1st February 2020

- TO DO LIST -

- [ ]
- [ ]
- [ ]
- [ ]
- [ ]

- NOTES -

February 2020

Sunday	Monday	Tuesday	Wednesday
26	27	28	29
2	3	4	5
9	10	11	12
16	17 *- Presidents' Day -*	18	19
23	24	25	26

"Happiness is not something ready made.
It comes from your own actions."
Dalai Lama XIV

Thursday	Friday	Saturday
30	31	1
6	7	8
13	14 - Valentine's Day -	15
20	21	22
27	28	29

- NOTES -

FEBRUARY 2020

S	M	T	W	T	F	S
26	27	28	29	30	31	1
2	3	4	5	6	7	8
9	10	11	12	13	14	15
16	17	18	19	20	21	22
23	24	25	26	27	28	29
1	2	3	4	5	6	7

14 Valentine's Day
17 Presidents' Day

- THIS WEEK NOTES -

- FOCUS LIST ON THE WEEK -

☐ ....
☐ ....
☐ ....

SUN • 2nd February 2020

- TO DO LIST -

☐
☐
☐
☐
☐

- NOTES -

MON • 3rd February 2020

- TO DO LIST -

☐
☐
☐
☐
☐

- NOTES -

TUE • 4th February 2020

- TO DO LIST -

☐
☐
☐
☐
☐

- NOTES -

WED • 5th February 2020

- TO DO LIST -

- [ ]
- [ ]
- [ ]
- [ ]
- [ ]

THU • 6th February 2020

- TO DO LIST -

- [ ]
- [ ]
- [ ]
- [ ]
- [ ]

- NOTES -

FRI • 7th February 2020

- TO DO LIST -

- [ ]
- [ ]
- [ ]
- [ ]
- [ ]

- NOTES -

SAT • 8th February 2020

- TO DO LIST -

- [ ]
- [ ]
- [ ]
- [ ]
- [ ]

- NOTES -

FEBRUARY 2020

S	M	T	W	T	F	S
26	27	28	29	30	31	1
2	3	4	5	6	7	8
9	10	11	12	13	14	15
16	17	18	19	20	21	22
23	24	25	26	27	28	29
1	2	3	4	5	6	7

14 Valentine's Day
17 Presidents' Day

- THIS WEEK NOTES -

- FOCUS LIST ON THE WEEK -

☐
☐
☐

SUN • 9th February 2020

- TO DO LIST -

☐
☐
☐
☐
☐

- NOTES -

MON • 10th February 2020

- TO DO LIST -

☐
☐
☐
☐
☐

- NOTES -

TUE • 11th February 2020

- TO DO LIST -

☐
☐
☐
☐
☐

- NOTES -

WED • 12th February 2020

- TO DO LIST -

☐
☐
☐
☐
☐

THU • 13th February 2020

- TO DO LIST -

☐
☐
☐
☐
☐

FRI • 14th February 2020

• Valentine's Day

- TO DO LIST -

☐
☐
☐
☐
☐

SAT • 15th February 2020

- TO DO LIST -

☐
☐
☐
☐
☐

FEBRUARY 2020

S	M	T	W	T	F	S
26	27	28	29	30	31	1
2	3	4	5	6	7	8
9	10	11	12	13	14	15
16	17	18	19	20	21	22
23	24	25	26	27	28	29
1	2	3	4	5	6	7

14 Valentine's Day
17 Presidents' Day

- THIS WEEK NOTES -

- FOCUS LIST ON THE WEEK -

- NOTES -

SUN • 16th February 2020

- TO DO LIST -

- NOTES -

MON • 17th February 2020

• Presidents' Day

- TO DO LIST -

- NOTES -

TUE • 18th February 2020

- TO DO LIST -

WED • 19th February 2020

- TO DO LIST -

- [ ]
- [ ]
- [ ]
- [ ]
- [ ]

THU • 20th February 2020

- TO DO LIST -

- [ ]
- [ ]
- [ ]
- [ ]
- [ ]

- NOTES -

FRI • 21st February 2020

- TO DO LIST -

- [ ]
- [ ]
- [ ]
- [ ]
- [ ]

- NOTES -

SAT • 22nd February 2020

- TO DO LIST -

- [ ]
- [ ]
- [ ]
- [ ]
- [ ]

- NOTES -

FEBRUARY 2020

S	M	T	W	T	F	S
26	27	28	29	30	31	1
2	3	4	5	6	7	8
9	10	11	12	13	14	15
16	17	18	19	20	21	22
23	24	25	26	27	28	29
1	2	3	4	5	6	7

14 Valentine's Day
17 Presidents' Day

- NOTES -

SUN • 23rd February 2020

- TO DO LIST -

- NOTES -

MON • 24th February 2020

- TO DO LIST -

- NOTES -

TUE • 25th February 2020

- TO DO LIST -

WED • 26th February 2020

- TO DO LIST -

☐
☐
☐
☐
☐

THU • 27th February 2020

- TO DO LIST -

☐
☐
☐
☐
☐

FRI • 28th February 2020

- TO DO LIST -

☐
☐
☐
☐
☐

SAT • 29th February 2020

- TO DO LIST -

☐
☐
☐
☐
☐

March 2020

Sunday	Monday	Tuesday	Wednesday
1	2	3	4
8	9	10	11
15	16	17 - St. Patrick's Day -	18
22	23	24	25
29	30	31	1

"What lies behind us and what lies before us are tiny matters
compared to what lies within us."
Ralph Waldo Emerson

Thursday	Friday	Saturday
5	6	7
12	13	14
19	20	21
26	27	28
2	3	4

- NOTES -

MARCH 2020

S	M	T	W	T	F	S
1	2	3	4	5	6	7
8	9	10	11	12	13	14
15	16	17	18	19	20	21
22	23	24	25	26	27	28
29	30	31	1	2	3	4
5	6	7	8	9	10	11

17 St. Patrick's Day

- THIS WEEK NOTES -

- FOCUS LIST ON THE WEEK -

- NOTES -

SUN • 1st March 2020

- TO DO LIST -

- NOTES -

MON • 2nd March 2020

- TO DO LIST -

- NOTES -

TUE • 3rd March 2020

- TO DO LIST -

WED • 4th March 2020

- TO DO LIST -

☐ _____
☐ _____
☐ _____
☐ _____
☐ _____

_____
_____
_____
_____
_____
_____
_____
_____
_____

THU • 5th March 2020

- TO DO LIST -

☐ _____
☐ _____
☐ _____
☐ _____
☐ _____

- NOTES -

_____
_____
_____
_____
_____
_____
_____
_____

FRI • 6th March 2020

- TO DO LIST -

☐ _____
☐ _____
☐ _____
☐ _____
☐ _____

- NOTES -

_____
_____
_____
_____
_____
_____
_____
_____

SAT • 7th March 2020

- TO DO LIST -

☐ _____
☐ _____
☐ _____
☐ _____
☐ _____

- NOTES -

_____
_____
_____
_____
_____
_____
_____
_____

MARCH 2020

S	M	T	W	T	F	S
1	2	3	4	5	6	7
8	9	10	11	12	13	14
15	16	17	18	19	20	21
22	23	24	25	26	27	28
29	30	31	1	2	3	4
5	6	7	8	9	10	11

17 St. Patrick's Day

- THIS WEEK NOTES -

- FOCUS LIST ON THE WEEK -

☐
☐
☐

SUN • 8th March 2020

- TO DO LIST -

☐
☐
☐
☐
☐

- NOTES -

MON • 9th March 2020

- TO DO LIST -

☐
☐
☐
☐
☐

- NOTES -

TUE • 10th March 2020

- TO DO LIST -

☐
☐
☐
☐
☐

- NOTES -

WED • 11th March 2020

- TO DO LIST -

- [ ]
- [ ]
- [ ]
- [ ]
- [ ]

THU • 12th March 2020

- NOTES -

- TO DO LIST -

- [ ]
- [ ]
- [ ]
- [ ]
- [ ]

FRI • 13th March 2020

- NOTES -

- TO DO LIST -

- [ ]
- [ ]
- [ ]
- [ ]
- [ ]

SAT • 14th March 2020

- NOTES -

- TO DO LIST -

- [ ]
- [ ]
- [ ]
- [ ]
- [ ]

MARCH 2020

S	M	T	W	T	F	S
1	2	3	4	5	6	7
8	9	10	11	12	13	14
15	16	17	18	19	20	21
22	23	24	25	26	27	28
29	30	31	1	2	3	4
5	6	7	8	9	10	11

17 St. Patrick's Day

- THIS WEEK NOTES -

- FOCUS LIST ON THE WEEK -

☐ _____

☐ _____

☐ _____

SUN • 15th March 2020

- TO DO LIST -

☐ _____
☐ _____
☐ _____
☐ _____
☐ _____

- NOTES -

MON • 16th March 2020

- TO DO LIST -

☐ _____
☐ _____
☐ _____
☐ _____
☐ _____

- NOTES -

TUE • 17th March 2020

• St. Patrick's Day

- TO DO LIST -

☐ _____
☐ _____
☐ _____
☐ _____
☐ _____

- NOTES -

WED • 18th March 2020

- TO DO LIST -

- [ ]
- [ ]
- [ ]
- [ ]
- [ ]

THU • 19th March 2020

- TO DO LIST -

- [ ]
- [ ]
- [ ]
- [ ]
- [ ]

FRI • 20th March 2020

- TO DO LIST -

- [ ]
- [ ]
- [ ]
- [ ]
- [ ]

SAT • 21st March 2020

- TO DO LIST -

- [ ]
- [ ]
- [ ]
- [ ]
- [ ]

MARCH 2020

S	M	T	W	T	F	S
1	2	3	4	5	6	7
8	9	10	11	12	13	14
15	16	17	18	19	20	21
22	23	24	25	26	27	28
29	30	31	1	2	3	4
5	6	7	8	9	10	11

17 St. Patrick's Day

- THIS WEEK NOTES -

- FOCUS LIST ON THE WEEK -

☐ ....
☐ ....
☐ ....

- NOTES -

SUN • 22nd March 2020

- TO DO LIST -

☐ ....
☐ ....
☐ ....
☐ ....
☐ ....

- NOTES -

MON • 23rd March 2020

- TO DO LIST -

☐ ....
☐ ....
☐ ....
☐ ....
☐ ....

- NOTES -

TUE • 24th March 2020

- TO DO LIST -

☐ ....
☐ ....
☐ ....
☐ ....
☐ ....

WED • 25th March 2020

- TO DO LIST -

- [ ]
- [ ]
- [ ]
- [ ]
- [ ]

- NOTES -

THU • 26th March 2020

- TO DO LIST -

- [ ]
- [ ]
- [ ]
- [ ]
- [ ]

- NOTES -

FRI • 27th March 2020

- TO DO LIST -

- [ ]
- [ ]
- [ ]
- [ ]
- [ ]

- NOTES -

SAT • 28th March 2020

- TO DO LIST -

- [ ]
- [ ]
- [ ]
- [ ]
- [ ]

- NOTES -

MARCH 2020

S	M	T	W	T	F	S
1	2	3	4	5	6	7
8	9	10	11	12	13	14
15	16	17	18	19	20	21
22	23	24	25	26	27	28
29	30	31	1	2	3	4
5	6	7	8	9	10	11

17 St. Patrick's Day

- THIS WEEK NOTES -

- FOCUS LIST ON THE WEEK -

☐
☐
☐

SUN • 29th March 2020

- TO DO LIST -

☐
☐
☐
☐
☐

- NOTES -

MON • 30th March 2020

- TO DO LIST -

☐
☐
☐
☐
☐

- NOTES -

TUE • 31st March 2020

- TO DO LIST -

☐
☐
☐
☐
☐

- NOTES -

WED • 1st April 2020

• April Fools' Day

- TO DO LIST -

☐ ....
☐ ....
☐ ....
☐ ....
☐ ....

- NOTES -

THU • 2nd April 2020

- TO DO LIST -

☐ ....
☐ ....
☐ ....
☐ ....
☐ ....

- NOTES -

FRI • 3rd April 2020

- TO DO LIST -

☐ ....
☐ ....
☐ ....
☐ ....
☐ ....

- NOTES -

SAT • 4th April 2020

- TO DO LIST -

☐ ....
☐ ....
☐ ....
☐ ....
☐ ....

- NOTES -

April 2020

Sunday	Monday	Tuesday	Wednesday
29	30	31	1 - April Fools' Day -
5	6	7	8
12	13	14	15
19	20	21	22
26	27	28	29

Thursday	Friday	Saturday
2	3	4
9	10	11
16	17	18
23	24	25
30	1	2

- NOTES -

....
....
....
....
....
....
....
....
....
....
....
....
....
....
....
....
....
....
....
....

APRIL 2020

S	M	T	W	T	F	S
29	30	31	1	2	3	4
5	6	7	8	9	10	11
12	13	14	15	16	17	18
19	20	21	22	23	24	25
26	27	28	29	30	1	2
3	4	5	6	7	8	9

1 April Fools' Day

- THIS WEEK NOTES -

- FOCUS LIST ON THE WEEK -

☐
☐
☐

- NOTES -

SUN • 5th April 2020

- TO DO LIST -

☐
☐
☐
☐
☐

- NOTES -

MON • 6th April 2020

- TO DO LIST -

☐
☐
☐
☐
☐

- NOTES -

TUE • 7th April 2020

- TO DO LIST -

☐
☐
☐
☐
☐

WED • 8th April 2020

- TO DO LIST -

- [ ]
- [ ]
- [ ]
- [ ]
- [ ]

THU • 9th April 2020

- NOTES -

- TO DO LIST -

- [ ]
- [ ]
- [ ]
- [ ]
- [ ]

FRI • 10th April 2020

- NOTES -

- TO DO LIST -

- [ ]
- [ ]
- [ ]
- [ ]
- [ ]

SAT • 11th April 2020

- NOTES -

- TO DO LIST -

- [ ]
- [ ]
- [ ]
- [ ]
- [ ]

APRIL 2020

S	M	T	W	T	F	S
29	30	31	1	2	3	4
5	6	7	8	9	10	11
12	13	14	15	16	17	18
19	20	21	22	23	24	25
26	27	28	29	30	1	2
3	4	5	6	7	8	9

1 April Fools' Day

- THIS WEEK NOTES -

- FOCUS LIST ON THE WEEK -

☐
☐
☐

SUN • 12th April 2020

- TO DO LIST -

☐
☐
☐
☐
☐

- NOTES -

MON • 13th April 2020

- TO DO LIST -

☐
☐
☐
☐
☐

- NOTES -

TUE • 14th April 2020

- TO DO LIST -

☐
☐
☐
☐
☐

- NOTES -

WED • 15th April 2020

- TO DO LIST -

- [ ]
- [ ]
- [ ]
- [ ]
- [ ]

THU • 16th April 2020

- TO DO LIST -

- [ ]
- [ ]
- [ ]
- [ ]
- [ ]

- NOTES -

FRI • 17th April 2020

- TO DO LIST -

- [ ]
- [ ]
- [ ]
- [ ]
- [ ]

- NOTES -

SAT • 18th April 2020

- TO DO LIST -

- [ ]
- [ ]
- [ ]
- [ ]
- [ ]

- NOTES -

APRIL 2020

S	M	T	W	T	F	S
29	30	31	1	2	3	4
5	6	7	8	9	10	11
12	13	14	15	16	17	18
19	20	21	22	23	24	25
26	27	28	29	30	1	2
3	4	5	6	7	8	9

1 April Fools' Day

- THIS WEEK NOTES -

- FOCUS LIST ON THE WEEK -

☐ _____
☐ _____
☐ _____

SUN • 19th April 2020

- TO DO LIST -

☐ _____
☐ _____
☐ _____
☐ _____
☐ _____

- NOTES -

MON • 20th April 2020

- TO DO LIST -

☐ _____
☐ _____
☐ _____
☐ _____
☐ _____

- NOTES -

TUE • 21st April 2020

- TO DO LIST -

☐ _____
☐ _____
☐ _____
☐ _____
☐ _____

- NOTES -

WED • 22nd April 2020

- TO DO LIST -

- [ ]
- [ ]
- [ ]
- [ ]
- [ ]

THU • 23rd April 2020

- NOTES -

- TO DO LIST -

- [ ]
- [ ]
- [ ]
- [ ]
- [ ]

FRI • 24th April 2020

- NOTES -

- TO DO LIST -

- [ ]
- [ ]
- [ ]
- [ ]
- [ ]

SAT • 25th April 2020

- NOTES -

- TO DO LIST -

- [ ]
- [ ]
- [ ]
- [ ]
- [ ]

APRIL 2020

S	M	T	W	T	F	S
29	30	31	1	2	3	4
5	6	7	8	9	10	11
12	13	14	15	16	17	18
19	20	21	22	23	24	25
26	27	28	29	30	1	2
3	4	5	6	7	8	9

1 April Fools' Day

- THIS WEEK NOTES -

- FOCUS LIST ON THE WEEK -

☐
☐
☐

SUN • 26th April 2020

- TO DO LIST -

☐
☐
☐
☐
☐

- NOTES -

MON • 27th April 2020

- TO DO LIST -

☐
☐
☐
☐
☐

- NOTES -

TUE • 28th April 2020

- TO DO LIST -

☐
☐
☐
☐
☐

- NOTES -

WED • 29th April 2020

- NOTES -

- TO DO LIST -

☐
☐
☐
☐
☐

THU • 30th April 2020

- NOTES -

- TO DO LIST -

☐
☐
☐
☐
☐

FRI • 1st May 2020

- NOTES -

- TO DO LIST -

☐
☐
☐
☐
☐

SAT • 2nd May 2020

- NOTES -

- TO DO LIST -

☐
☐
☐
☐
☐

May 2020

Sunday	Monday	Tuesday	Wednesday
26	27	28	29
3	4	5	6
10 - Mother's Day -	11	12	13
17	18	19	20
24 31	25 - Memorial Day -	26	27

"It is better in prayer to have a heart without words
than words without a heart."
Mahatma Gandhi

Thursday	Friday	Saturday
30	1	2
7	8	9
14	15	16
21	22	23
28	29	30

- NOTES -

MAY 2020

S	M	T	W	T	F	S
26	27	28	29	30	1	2
3	4	5	6	7	8	9
10	11	12	13	14	15	16
17	18	19	20	21	22	23
24	25	26	27	28	29	30
31	1	2	3	4	5	6

10 Mother's Day
25 Memorial Day

- THIS WEEK NOTES -

- FOCUS LIST ON THE WEEK -

☐ _____
☐ _____
☐ _____

SUN • 3rd May 2020

- TO DO LIST -

☐ _____
☐ _____
☐ _____
☐ _____
☐ _____

- NOTES -

MON • 4th May 2020

- TO DO LIST -

☐ _____
☐ _____
☐ _____
☐ _____
☐ _____

- NOTES -

TUE • 5th May 2020

- TO DO LIST -

☐ _____
☐ _____
☐ _____
☐ _____
☐ _____

- NOTES -

WED • 6th May 2020

- TO DO LIST -

☐ _____
☐ _____
☐ _____
☐ _____
☐ _____

THU • 7th May 2020

- TO DO LIST -

☐ _____
☐ _____
☐ _____
☐ _____
☐ _____

- NOTES -

FRI • 8th May 2020

- TO DO LIST -

☐ _____
☐ _____
☐ _____
☐ _____
☐ _____

- NOTES -

SAT • 9th May 2020

- TO DO LIST -

☐ _____
☐ _____
☐ _____
☐ _____
☐ _____

- NOTES -

MAY 2020

S	M	T	W	T	F	S
26	27	28	29	30	1	2
3	4	5	6	7	8	9
10	11	12	13	14	15	16
17	18	19	20	21	22	23
24	25	26	27	28	29	30
31	1	2	3	4	5	6

10 Mother's Day
25 Memorial Day

- THIS WEEK NOTES -

- FOCUS LIST ON THE WEEK -

SUN • 10th May 2020

• Mother's Day

- TO DO LIST -

- NOTES -

MON • 11th May 2020

- TO DO LIST -

- NOTES -

TUE • 12th May 2020

- TO DO LIST -

- NOTES -

WED • 13th May 2020

- TO DO LIST -

- [ ] _____
- [ ] _____
- [ ] _____
- [ ] _____
- [ ] _____

THU • 14th May 2020

- TO DO LIST -

- [ ] _____
- [ ] _____
- [ ] _____
- [ ] _____
- [ ] _____

- NOTES -

FRI • 15th May 2020

- TO DO LIST -

- [ ] _____
- [ ] _____
- [ ] _____
- [ ] _____
- [ ] _____

- NOTES -

SAT • 16th May 2020

- TO DO LIST -

- [ ] _____
- [ ] _____
- [ ] _____
- [ ] _____
- [ ] _____

- NOTES -

MAY 2020

S	M	T	W	T	F	S
26	27	28	29	30	1	2
3	4	5	6	7	8	9
10	11	12	13	14	15	16
17	18	19	20	21	22	23
24	25	26	27	28	29	30
31	1	2	3	4	5	6

10 Mother's Day
25 Memorial Day

- THIS WEEK NOTES -

- FOCUS LIST ON THE WEEK -

- NOTES -

SUN • 17th May 2020

- TO DO LIST -

- NOTES -

MON • 18th May 2020

- TO DO LIST -

- NOTES -

TUE • 19th May 2020

- TO DO LIST -

WED • 20th May 2020

- TO DO LIST -

- [ ]
- [ ]
- [ ]
- [ ]
- [ ]

- NOTES -

THU • 21st May 2020

- TO DO LIST -

- [ ]
- [ ]
- [ ]
- [ ]
- [ ]

- NOTES -

FRI • 22nd May 2020

- TO DO LIST -

- [ ]
- [ ]
- [ ]
- [ ]
- [ ]

- NOTES -

SAT • 23rd May 2020

- TO DO LIST -

- [ ]
- [ ]
- [ ]
- [ ]
- [ ]

- NOTES -

MAY 2020

S	M	T	W	T	F	S
26	27	28	29	30	1	2
3	4	5	6	7	8	9
10	11	12	13	14	15	16
17	18	19	20	21	22	23
24	25	26	27	28	29	30
31	1	2	3	4	5	6

10 Mother's Day
25 Memorial Day

- THIS WEEK NOTES -

- FOCUS LIST ON THE WEEK -

☐
☐
☐

SUN • 24th May 2020

- TO DO LIST -

☐
☐
☐
☐
☐

- NOTES -

MON • 25th May 2020

• Memorial Day

- TO DO LIST -

☐
☐
☐
☐
☐

- NOTES -

TUE • 26th May 2020

- TO DO LIST -

☐
☐
☐
☐
☐

- NOTES -

WED • 27th May 2020

- TO DO LIST -

- [ ]
- [ ]
- [ ]
- [ ]
- [ ]

THU • 28th May 2020

- TO DO LIST -

- [ ]
- [ ]
- [ ]
- [ ]
- [ ]

FRI • 29th May 2020

- TO DO LIST -

- [ ]
- [ ]
- [ ]
- [ ]
- [ ]

SAT • 30th May 2020

- TO DO LIST -

- [ ]
- [ ]
- [ ]
- [ ]
- [ ]

MAY 2020

S	M	T	W	T	F	S
26	27	28	29	30	1	2
3	4	5	6	7	8	9
10	11	12	13	14	15	16
17	18	19	20	21	22	23
24	25	26	27	28	29	30
31	1	2	3	4	5	6

10 Mother's Day
25 Memorial Day

- THIS WEEK NOTES -

- FOCUS LIST ON THE WEEK -
- [ ]
- [ ]
- [ ]

- NOTES -

SUN • 31st May 2020

- TO DO LIST -
- [ ]
- [ ]
- [ ]
- [ ]
- [ ]

- NOTES -

MON • 1st June 2020

- TO DO LIST -
- [ ]
- [ ]
- [ ]
- [ ]
- [ ]

- NOTES -

TUE • 2nd June 2020

- TO DO LIST -
- [ ]
- [ ]
- [ ]
- [ ]
- [ ]

WED • 3rd June 2020

- TO DO LIST -

☐ _____
☐ _____
☐ _____
☐ _____
☐ _____

- NOTES -

_____
_____
_____
_____
_____
_____
_____
_____

THU • 4th June 2020

- TO DO LIST -

☐ _____
☐ _____
☐ _____
☐ _____
☐ _____

- NOTES -

_____
_____
_____
_____
_____
_____
_____
_____

FRI • 5th June 2020

- TO DO LIST -

☐ _____
☐ _____
☐ _____
☐ _____
☐ _____

- NOTES -

_____
_____
_____
_____
_____
_____
_____
_____

SAT • 6th June 2020

- TO DO LIST -

☐ _____
☐ _____
☐ _____
☐ _____
☐ _____

- NOTES -

_____
_____
_____
_____
_____
_____
_____
_____

June 2020

Sunday	Monday	Tuesday	Wednesday
31	1	2	3
7	8	9	10
14	15	16	17
21 - Father's Day -	22	23	24
28	29	30	1

"The future belongs to those who believe in the beauty of their dreams."

Eleanor Roosevelt

Thursday	Friday	Saturday
4	5	6
11	12	13
18	19	20
25	26	27
2	3	4

- NOTES -

....
....
....
....
....
....
....
....
....
....
....
....
....
....
....
....
....
....
....
....
....
....
....
....
....

JUNE 2020

S	M	T	W	T	F	S
31	1	2	3	4	5	6
7	8	9	10	11	12	13
14	15	16	17	18	19	20
21	22	23	24	25	26	27
28	29	30	1	2	3	4
5	6	7	8	9	10	11

21 Father's Day

- THIS WEEK NOTES -

- FOCUS LIST ON THE WEEK -
☐
☐
☐

SUN • 7th June 2020

- TO DO LIST -

☐
☐
☐
☐
☐

- NOTES -

MON • 8th June 2020

- TO DO LIST -

☐
☐
☐
☐
☐

- NOTES -

TUE • 9th June 2020

- TO DO LIST -

☐
☐
☐
☐
☐

- NOTES -

WED • 10th June 2020

- TO DO LIST -

- [ ]
- [ ]
- [ ]
- [ ]
- [ ]

THU • 11th June 2020

- TO DO LIST -

- [ ]
- [ ]
- [ ]
- [ ]
- [ ]

FRI • 12th June 2020

- TO DO LIST -

- [ ]
- [ ]
- [ ]
- [ ]
- [ ]

SAT • 13th June 2020

- TO DO LIST -

- [ ]
- [ ]
- [ ]
- [ ]
- [ ]

JUNE 2020

S	M	T	W	T	F	S
31	1	2	3	4	5	6
7	8	9	10	11	12	13
14	15	16	17	18	19	20
21	22	23	24	25	26	27
28	29	30	1	2	3	4
5	6	7	8	9	10	11

21 Father's Day

- THIS WEEK NOTES -

- FOCUS LIST ON THE WEEK -

☐
☐
☐

SUN • 14th June 2020

- TO DO LIST -

☐
☐
☐
☐
☐

- NOTES -

MON • 15th June 2020

- TO DO LIST -

☐
☐
☐
☐
☐

- NOTES -

TUE • 16th June 2020

- TO DO LIST -

☐
☐
☐
☐
☐

- NOTES -

WED • 17th June 2020

- TO DO LIST -

☐
☐
☐
☐
☐

THU • 18th June 2020

- TO DO LIST -

☐
☐
☐
☐
☐

- NOTES -

FRI • 19th June 2020

- TO DO LIST -

☐
☐
☐
☐
☐

- NOTES -

SAT • 20th June 2020

- TO DO LIST -

☐
☐
☐
☐
☐

- NOTES -

JUNE 2020

S	M	T	W	T	F	S
31	1	2	3	4	5	6
7	8	9	10	11	12	13
14	15	16	17	18	19	20
21	22	23	24	25	26	27
28	29	30	1	2	3	4
5	6	7	8	9	10	11

21 Father's Day

- THIS WEEK NOTES -

- FOCUS LIST ON THE WEEK -
- ☐ ....
- ☐ ....
- ☐ ....

SUN • 21st June 2020

• Father's Day

- TO DO LIST -

☐ ....
☐ ....
☐ ....
☐ ....
☐ ....

- NOTES -

MON • 22nd June 2020

- TO DO LIST -

☐ ....
☐ ....
☐ ....
☐ ....
☐ ....

- NOTES -

TUE • 23rd June 2020

- TO DO LIST -

☐ ....
☐ ....
☐ ....
☐ ....
☐ ....

- NOTES -

WED • 24th June 2020

- TO DO LIST -

☐
☐
☐
☐
☐

- NOTES -

THU • 25th June 2020

- TO DO LIST -

☐
☐
☐
☐
☐

- NOTES -

FRI • 26th June 2020

- TO DO LIST -

☐
☐
☐
☐
☐

- NOTES -

SAT • 27th June 2020

- TO DO LIST -

☐
☐
☐
☐
☐

- NOTES -

JUNE 2020

S	M	T	W	T	F	S
31	1	2	3	4	5	6
7	8	9	10	11	12	13
14	15	16	17	18	19	20
21	22	23	24	25	26	27
28	29	30	1	2	3	4
5	6	7	8	9	10	11

21 Father's Day

- THIS WEEK NOTES -

- FOCUS LIST ON THE WEEK -

☐ ----------------------
☐ ----------------------
☐ ----------------------

SUN • 28th June 2020

- TO DO LIST -

☐
☐
☐
☐
☐

- NOTES -

MON • 29th June 2020

- TO DO LIST -

☐
☐
☐
☐
☐

- NOTES -

TUE • 30th June 2020

- TO DO LIST -

☐
☐
☐
☐
☐

- NOTES -

WED • 1st July 2020

- TO DO LIST -

☐
☐
☐
☐
☐

- NOTES -

THU • 2nd July 2020

- TO DO LIST -

☐
☐
☐
☐
☐

- NOTES -

FRI • 3rd July 2020

- TO DO LIST -

☐
☐
☐
☐
☐

- NOTES -

SAT • 4th July 2020

• Independence Day

- TO DO LIST -

☐
☐
☐
☐
☐

- NOTES -

Gratitude Moments

Made in the USA
Middletown, DE
05 November 2019